The Ultimate Guide to Hacking Made Easy

by Neo Monefa

Table of Contents

1. What is Hacking?

Hacking is any specialized push to control the typical conduct of system associations and associated frameworks. A hacker is any individual occupied with hacking. The expression "hacking" truly alluded to productive, shrewd specialized work that was not inexorably identified with PC frameworks. Today, be that as it may, hacking and hackers are most normally connected with malevolent hacking attacks on the Internet and different systems.

Amid the 1990s, the expression "hacker" initially meant a gifted software engineer capable in machine code and PC working frameworks. Specifically, these people could simply hack on an unsuitable framework to take care of issues and take part in a little hacking organization secret activities by translating a contender's code.

Lamentably, some of these hackers additionally got to be specialists at getting to secret word ensured PCs, records, and systems and came to known as "crackers". Obviously, a successful and unsafe "cracker" must be a decent hacker and the terms got to be interwoven. Hackers won out in mainstream use and in the media and today allude to any individual who plays out some type of PC harm.

2. Classification of Hackers

The expression "Hacker" is somebody who breaks into PC systems for the joy he gets from the test of doing it or with some different aims like taking information for cash or with political inspirations. Hackers are grouped to various sorts. Some of them are recorded underneath.

* White Hat: A White Hat hacker is a PC system security proficient and has non-malevolent motive at whatever point he breaks into security systems. A White Hat hacker has profound learning in Computer Networking, Network Protocols and System Administration (no less than three or four Operating Systems and great abilities in Scripting and Hacking). White Hat hacker has additionally great information in hacking instruments and knows how to program hacking devices.

A White Hat hacker has the right stuff to break into systems yet he utilizes his abilities to secure associations. A White Hat hacker can direct weakness evaluations and entrance tests are otherwise called an Ethical Hacker. Regularly White Hat hackers are utilized by organizations and associations to check the vulnerabilities of their system and ensure that no opening is accessible in their system for an interloper.

* Black Hat: A Black Hat hacker, otherwise called a saltine, is a PC proficient with profound learning in Computer Networking, Network Protocols and System Administration (no less than three or four Operating Systems and great abilities in Scripting and Hacking). Black Hat hacker has likewise great information in numerous hacking instruments and knows how to program hacking apparatuses. A Black Hat hacker utilizes his aptitudes for dishonest reasons. A Black Hat hacker dependably has vindictive goal for barging in a system. Case: To take research information from an organization, to take cash from charge cards, Hack Email Accounts and so forth.

* Grey Hat: A Grey Hat hacker is somebody who is between White Hat hacker and Black Hat hacker. Grey Hat ordinarily do the hacking without the authorizations from the chairmen of the system he is hacking. Be that as it may, he will uncover the system vulnerabilities to the system administrators and offer a fix for the weakness for cash.

* Script Kiddie: A Script Kiddie is essentially a hacker beginner who doesn't has much learning to program instruments to breaks into PC systems. He frequently utilizes downloaded hacking devices from web composed by different hackers/security specialists.

* Hacktivist: A Hacktivist is a hacker with political aims. The hacktivist has the same aptitudes as that of a hacker and utilizes the same applications as the hacker. The essential expectation of a hacktivist is to convey open consideration regarding a political matter.

* Phreaker: Phreaker is a telecom system hacker who hacks a phone framework wrongfully to make calls without paying for them.

3. Hack Attacks & Tools

Types of Attacks:

*   Trojan programs that share information through instant messenger.

*   Phishing

*   Fake Websites.

*   IP/Server Spoofing

*   Trojan Horses

*   Electronic Bulletin Boards

*   Information Brokers

*   Wormhole Attack

*   Spyware

*   Internet Public Records

*   DNS Poisoning

Hacking Tools:

*   John The Ripper

John the Ripper (regularly you'll see truncated as 'JTR') wins the grant for having the coolest name. John the Ripper, generally just knows as, "John" is a well known password breaking pentesting instrument that is most regularly used to perform lexicon attacks. John the Ripper takes content string tests (from a content record, alluded to as a 'wordlist', containing well known and complex words found in a lexicon or genuine passwords broke before), scrambling it similarly as the watchword being split (counting both the encryption calculation and key), and contrasting the yield with the encoded string. This device can likewise be utilized to play out an assortment of changes to word reference attacks. On the off chance that you are to some degree befuddled between John the Ripper and THC Hydra then consider John the Ripper as an "offline" password cracker while THC Hydra is an "online" cracker.

*   Wireshark

Wireshark is an extremely mainstream pentesting software. Wireshark basically catches information bundles in a system progressively and after that shows the information in intelligible organization (verbose). The apparatus (stage) has been exceptionally created and it incorporates channels, shading coding and different components that gives the client a chance to delve profound into system movement and assess singular bundles. On the off chance that you'd like to wind up an infiltration analyzer or work as a Cyber Security practioner, then figuring out how to utilize Wireshark is an unquestionable requirement. There are huge amounts of assets out there to learn Wireshark, and, exceptionally compelling, there's additionally a Wireshark Certification which you can accomplish and put on your LinkedIn profile.

* Cain and Abel Hacking Tool

Cain and Abel (also known as Cain) is an enormously prevalent hacking device and one that is all the time specified online in an assortment of 'hacking instructional exercises'. At its heart, Cain and Abel is a secret word recuperation device for Microsoft Windows yet it can be utilized off-mark as a part of an assortment of employments, for instance, white and black cap hackers use Cain to recoup (i.e. 'crack') numerous sorts of passwords utilizing techniques, for example, system parcel sniffing and by utilizing the instrument to split secret key hashes. Cain, for instance, when used to break password hashes would utilize techniques, for example, rainbow table attacks, dictionary attacks, brute force and cryptanalysis attacks.

* Nmap (Network Mapper)

Nmap is a shortening of 'Network Mapper', and it's exceptionally notable free open source hackers device. Nmap is primarily utilized for system disclosure and security examining. Actually, a great many framework administrators all around the globe will utilize nmap for system stock, check for open ports, oversee administration redesign calendars, and screen host or administration uptime. Nmap, as an apparatus utilizes crude IP bundles as a part of innovative approaches to figure out what hosts are accessible on the system, what administrations (application name and form) those hosts are giving data about, what working frameworks (fingerprinting) and what sort and form of parcel channels/firewalls are being utilized by the objective. There are many advantages of utilizing nmap, one of which is that reality that the administrator client can figure out if the system (and related hubs) needs fixing. Nmap's been included in actually every hacker motion picture out there, not slightest the late Mr. Robot arrangement. It's likewise worth specifying that there's a GUI form of Nmap called 'Zenmap'. We'd encourage you to learn utilizing Nmap (i.e. the 'summon line') then pivot into Zenmap when you are feeling all sure.

* Metasploit Penetration Testing Software

The Metasploit Project is an immensely famous pentesting or hacking structure. On the off chance that you are new to Metasploit consider it a 'gathering of hacking devices and structures' that can be utilized to execute different assignments. Broadly utilized by cybersecurity experts and moral hackers this is an instrument that you need to learn. Metasploit is basically a PC security venture (system) that gives the client crucial data with respect to known security vulnerabilities and figures entrance testing and IDS testing arrangements, procedures and strategies for abuse. There's a huge amount of extraordinarily valuable Metasploit data out there and we trust that the books that we've picked go some way to help you on your excursion, not minimum on the off chance that you are an apprentice simply beginning and searching for amateurs instructional exercises in how to utilize Metasploit.

4. Malware

Malware is a condensed term signifying "malicious software". This is a software that is particularly intended to obtain entrance or harm a PC without the learning of the proprietor. There are different sorts of malware including keyloggers, spyware, true viruses, worms, or any kind of pernicious code that invades a PC. By and large, hacking is considered malware taking into account the plan of the maker as opposed to its real components. Malware creation is on the ascent because of the sheer volume of new sorts made day by day and the bait of cash that can be made through composed web wrongdoing. Malware was initially made as investigations and tricks, yet in the long run prompted vandalism and decimation of focused machines. Today, a lot of malware is made for benefit through constrained promoting (adware), taking delicate data (spyware), spreading email spam or tyke erotica (zombie computers), or to blackmail cash (ransomware). Different elements can make PCs more defenseless against malware attacks, incorporating abandons in the working framework plan, having the majority of the PCs on a system run the same OS, offering clients to much consents or simply utilizing the Windows OS (because of its notoriety, it gets the most malware composed for it).

Types of Malware:

Adware: The minimum hazardous and most lucrative Malware. Adware shows advertisements on your PC.

Spyware: Spyware is hacking that spies on you, following your web exercises keeping in mind the end goal to send promoting (Adware) back to your framework.

Virus: An virus is an infectious program or code that connects itself to another bit of application, and afterward repeats itself when that product is run. Regularly this is spread by sharing hacking or records between PCs.

Worm: A system that recreates itself and obliterates information and records on the PC. Worms work to "eat" the framework working records and information documents until the drive is void.

Trojan: The most hazardous Malware. Trojans are composed with the reason for finding your money related data, assuming control over your PC's framework assets, and in bigger frameworks making a "dissent of-administration attack " Denial-of-administration attack: an endeavor to make a machine or system asset occupied to those endeavoring to achieve it. Illustration: AOL, Yahoo or your business system getting to be occupied.

Rootkit: This one is compared to the criminal stowing away in the storage room, holding up to take from you while you are not home. It is the hardest of all Malware to recognize and thus to evacuate; numerous specialists prescribe totally wiping your hard drive and reinstalling everything sans preparation. It is intended to allow the other data gathering Malware into get the personality data from your PC without you understanding anything is going on.

Backdoors: Backdoors are much the same as Trojans or worms, with the exception of that they open an "indirect access" onto a PC, giving a system association with hackers or other Malware to enter or for infections or SPAM to be sent.

Keyloggers: Records all that you write on your PC with a specific end goal to gather your log-in names, passwords, and other touchy data, and send it on to the wellspring of the keylogging program. Ordinarily keyloggers are utilized by enterprises and guardians to get PC utilization data.

Rogue security software: This one tricks or misdirects clients. It puts on a show to be a decent program to evacuate Malware diseases, yet at the same time it is the Malware. Regularly it will kill the genuine Anti-Virus hacking. The following picture demonstrates the common screen for this Malware program, Antivirus 2010

Ransomware: If you see this screen cautions you that you have been bolted out of your PC until you pay for your cybercrimes. Your framework is seriously contaminated with a type of Malware called Ransomware. It is not a genuine notice from the FBI, be that as it may, rather a contamination of the framework itself. Regardless of the fact that you pay to open the framework, the framework is opened, however you are not free of it locking you out once more. The solicitation for cash, more often than not in the many dollars is totally fake.

Browser Hijacker: When your landing page changes to one that resembles those in the pictures embedded next, you may have been tainted with some type of a Browser Hijacker. This unsafe Malware will divert your ordinary inquiry movement and give you the outcomes the engineers need you to see. It will likely profit off your web surfing. Utilizing this landing page and not evacuating the Malware gives the source engineers a chance to catch your surfing advantages. This is particularly hazardous when keeping money or shopping on the web. These landing pages can look innocuous, yet for each situation they permit other more irresistible

5. Attack Viruses

*   Resident Viruses

This sort of virus is a changeless which abides in the RAM memory. From that point it can overcome and interfere with the majority of the operations executed by the framework: tainting records and projects that are opened, shut, replicated, renamed and so forth.

Example: Randex, CMJ, Meve, and MrKlunky.

*   Multipartite Viruses

Multipartite viruses are dispersed through tainted media and for the most part cover up in the memory. Step by step, the virus moves to the boot part of the hard drive and taints executable documents on the hard drive and later over the PC framework.

*   Direct Action Viruses

The primary motivation behind this virus is to recreate and make a move when it is executed. At the point when a particular condition is met, the virus will go energetically and taint records in the index or envelope that it is in and in catalogs that are indicated in the AUTOEXEC.BAT document PATH. This cluster document is constantly situated in the root index of the hard plate and does certain operations when the PC is booted.

* Overwrite Viruses

Virus of this kind is described by the way that it erases the data contained in the records that it taints, rendering them in part or absolutely futile once they have been contaminated.

The best way to clean a record tainted by an overwrite virus is to erase the document totally, hence losing the first substance.

Examples: Way, Trj.Reboot, Trivial.88.D.

* Boot Virus

This kind of virus influences the boot area of a floppy or hard plate. This is a vital part of a circle, in which data on the plate itself is put away together with a project that makes it conceivable to boot (begin) the PC from the circle.

The most ideal method for evading boot viruses is to guarantee that floppy circles are compose secured and never begin your PC with an obscure floppy plate in the plate drive.

Example: Polyboot.B, AntiEXE.

* Macro Virus

Large scale viruses taint records that are made utilizing certain applications or projects that contain macros. These little projects make it conceivable to robotize arrangement of operations with the goal that they are executed as a solitary activity, in this manner sparing the client from carrying them out one by one.

Example: Relax, Melissa.A, Bablas, O97M/Y2K.

* Directory Virus

Catalog viruses change the ways that demonstrate the area of a record. By executing a system (record with the expansion .EXE or .COM) which has been tainted by a virus, you are unwittingly running the virus program, while the first document and program have been already moved by the virus.

Once contaminated it gets to be difficult to find the first records.

* Polymorphic Virus

Polymorphic viruses scramble or encode themselves in an unexpected way (utilizing diverse calculations and encryption keys) each time they taint a framework.

This makes it inconceivable for hostile to viruses to discover them utilizing string or mark seeks (since they are distinctive in every encryption) furthermore empowers them to make an extensive number of duplicates of themselves.

Example: Elkern, Marburg, Satan Bug, and Tuareg.

* File Infectors

This sort of virus contaminates programs or executable records (documents with an .EXE or .COM expansion). When one of these projects is run, specifically or in a roundabout way, the virus is actuated, creating the harming impacts it is modified to do. The greater part of existing viruses has a place with this classification, and can be ordered relying upon the activities that they do.

* Encrypted Viruses

This kind of viruses comprises of encoded pernicious code, unscrambled module. The viruses use scrambled code strategy which makes antivirus hacking scarcely to recognize them. The antivirus program more often than not can identify this kind of viruses when they attempt spread by unscrambled themselves.

* Companion Viruses

Sidekick viruses can be considered record infector viruses like occupant or direct activity sorts. They are known as sidekick viruses on the grounds that once they get into the framework they "go with" alternate records that as of now exist. At the end of the day, keeping in mind the end goal to do their contamination schedules, sidekick viruses can hold up in memory until a system is run (occupant viruses) or act promptly by making duplicates of themselves (direct activity viruses).

Example: Stator, Asimov.1539, and Terrax.1069

* Network Virus

System viruses quickly spread through a Local Network Area (LAN), and now and again all through the web. For the most part, system viruses duplicate through shared assets, i.e., shared drives and envelopes. At the point when the virus taints a PC, it seeks through the system to attack its new potential prey. At the point when the virus wraps up that PC, it proceeds onward to the following and the cycle rehashes itself.

Example: Nimda and SQLSlammer.

* Nonresident Viruses

This kind of viruses is like Resident Viruses by utilizing replication of module. Other than that, Nonresident Viruses part as discoverer module which can contaminate to records when it discovered one (it will choose one or more documents to taint every time the module is executed).

* Stealth Viruses

Stealth Viruses is some kind of viruses which attempt to trap hostile to virus hacking by blocking its solicitations to the working framework. It has capacity to conceal itself from some antivirus hacking programs. Along these lines, some antivirus program can't identify them.

* Sparce Infectors

With a specific end goal to spread broadly, a virus must endeavor to maintain a strategic distance from identification. To minimize the likelihood of its being found a virus could utilize any number of various methods. It may, for instance, just taint each twentieth time a record is executed; it may just contaminate documents whose lengths are inside barely characterized ranges or whose names start with letters in a specific scope of the letters in order. There are numerous different potential outcomes.

* Spacefiller (Cavity) Viruses

Numerous viruss take the path of least resistance when tainting documents; they essentially connect themselves to the end of the record and afterward change the start of the project so that it first indicates the virus and afterward to the real program code. Numerous viruses that do this likewise actualize some stealth methods so you don't see the expansion in document length when the virus is dynamic in memory.

A spacefiller (hole) virus, then again, endeavors to be smart. Some system records, for an assortment of reasons, have vacant space within them. This void space can be utilized to house virus code. A spacefiller virus endeavors to introduce itself in this unfilled space while not harming the real program itself. Leverage of this is the virus then does not expand the length of the project and can dodge the requirement for some stealth systems. The Lehigh virus was an early case of a spacefiller virus.

* FAT Virus

The document distribution table or FAT is the part of a circle used to interface data and is a fundamental part of the ordinary working of the PC.

This sort of virus attack can be particularly unsafe, by averting access to specific segments of the circle where imperative records are put away. Harm brought about can bring about data misfortunes from individual documents or even whole registries.

* Worms

A worm is in fact not a virus, but rather a project fundamentally the same as an virus; it can self-repeat, and can prompt negative impacts on your framework and in particular they are recognized and killed by antiviruses.

Example: PSWBugbear.B, Lovgate.F, Trile.C, Sobig.D, Mapson.

* Trojans or Trojan Horses

Another upsetting type of noxious code (not a virus also) are Trojans or Trojan steeds, which dissimilar to viruses don't imitate by contaminating different records, nor do they self-reproduce like worms.

* Logic Bombs

They are not considered viruses since they don't repeat. They are not programs in their own particular right yet rather covered portions of different projects.

Their goal is to decimate information on the PC once certain conditions have been met. Rationale bombs go undetected until propelled, and the outcomes can be damaging.

6. Masking Your IP Address

Reasons why individuals need to shroud their IP location would be to conceal their geographical area, prevent web following, to avoid leaving a digital footprint and to sidestep any bans or boycotting of their IP address.

A Trusted Proxy or Virtual Private Network can be used to hide IP address. Join with these administrations and when you go on the web, you'll be demonstrating the world with an alternate IP address, one that is on advance from the administration you're utilizing.

VPNs can be free or you can pay for the administration. They help you get on the Internet and relegate you an alternate IP address, however there's an extensive variety of unwavering quality in suppliers.

There are numerous more points of interest to utilizing an individual VPN administration over an intermediary (convenience, security, access to blocked locales).

Virtual Private Network (VPN) offers an availability to another system, and when associated your PC gets another IP address from a VPN supplier. Each movement from your PC courses through the VPN system, so your actual IP address doled out by your ISP is covered up. Beside concealing your IP address, utilizing VPN permits you to get to any system despite the fact that your system might be geo-limited. They help you get on the Internet with an alternate IP address than the one gave by your ISP.

Here are some VPN supplier cases:

- Express VPN

- Vypr VPN

- Pure VPN

On the other hand, you may utilize free Wi-Fi administrations offered by a coffee shop, lodging or any open areas. An IP address does not go with your PC, but rather they are somewhat alloted by the switch collocated in the region you are in.

7. Hacking Email

There are two most ideal ways, which are by utilizing Keylogger and Phising

*   Keylogger

How does a Keylogger Work?

A Keylogger is a software program that can without much of a stretch be introduced by any amateur PC client. Once introduced, it records every one of the keystrokes wrote on the PC including passwords. It doesn't require any extraordinary information or ability to utilize keyloggers.

Can a Keylogger be Detected?

No! Once introduced, it works in a complete stealth mode and consequently stays undetected to the PC client.

Consider the possibility that I don't have Physical Access to the Target Computer:

Nothing to worry about! A portion of the best keyloggers available bolster "remote installation" that makes it conceivable to introduce it regardless of the possibility that the objective PC is several miles away.

In what manner can a Keylogger Help Me in Hacking Email Password?

Once introduced, the keylogger essentially records every one of the keystrokes wrote (counting passwords) and transfers the logs to a mystery server. You can get to these logs at whatever time by signing into your online record that accompanies the keylogger program.

* Phishing

Phishing is the other most utilized method to hack email passwords. This technique includes the utilization of Fake Login Pages (ridiculed site pages) whose look and feel are verging on indistinguishable to that of genuine sites.

Fake login pages are made by numerous hackers which seem precisely as Gmail or Yahoo login pages. Be that as it may, once you enter your login points of interest on such a fake login page, they are really stolen away by the hacker.

Notwithstanding, completing a phishing attack requests a top to bottom mastery in the field of hacking. It requires years of involvement with information of HTML, CSS and scripting dialects like PHP/JSP.

Additionally, phishing is considered as a genuine crime and consequently an unsafe occupation to endeavor. In the event that you are a fledgling PC client, I suggest the use of keyloggers as the least demanding and most ideal approach to access any email password.

8. Spoofing Technique

What Is a Spoofing Attack?

A spoofing attack is the point at which a noxious gathering mimics another gadget or client on a system keeping in mind the end goal to dispatch attacks against system has, take information, spread malware or detour access controls. There are a few distinct sorts of ridiculing attacks that malignant gatherings can use to fulfill this. Probably the most widely recognized techniques incorporate IP address parodying attacks, ARP satirizing attacks and DNS server caricaturing attacks.

IP Address Spoofing Attacks

IP address spoofing is a standout amongst the most every now and again utilized spoofing attack techniques. In an IP address spoofing attack, an aggressor sends IP bundles from a false (or "caricature") source address so as to camouflage itself. Refusal of-administration attacks frequently utilize IP ridiculing to over-burden systems and gadgets with bundles that seem, by all accounts, to be from true blue source IP addresses.

There are two ways that IP spoofing attacks can be utilized to over-burden focuses with movement. One strategy is to just surge a chose focus with bundles from numerous satirize addresses. This strategy works by straightforwardly sending a casualty a bigger number of information than it can deal with. The other technique is to spoof the objective's IP address and send bundles from that location to a wide range of beneficiaries on the system. At the point when another machine gets a bundle, it will naturally transmit a parcel to the sender accordingly. Since the spoofed parcels give off an impression of being sent from the objective's IP address, all reactions to the spoofed packets will be sent to (and surge) the objective's IP address.

IP spoofing attacks can likewise be utilized to sidestep IP address-based confirmation. This procedure can be exceptionally troublesome and is fundamentally utilized when trust connections are as a part of spot between machines on a system and inner frameworks. Trust connections use IP addresses (as opposed to client logins) to confirm machines' characters when endeavoring to get to frameworks. This empowers malevolent gatherings to utilize spoofing attacks to mimic machines with access authorizations and detour trust-based system efforts to establish safety.

ARP Spoofing Attacks

ARP is short for Address Resolution Protocol, a protocol that is utilized to determine IP locations to MAC (Media Access Control) addresses for transmitting information. In an ARP spoofing attacks, a vindictive gathering sends spoofed ARP messages over a neighborhood keeping in mind the end goal to interface the aggressor's MAC address with the IP location of a genuine individual from the system. This sort of caricaturing attack brings about information that is planned for the host's IP address getting sent to the attacker. Pernicious gatherings ordinarily utilize ARP parodying to take data, alter information in-travel or stop activity on a LAN. ARP spoofing attacks can likewise be utilized to encourage different sorts of attacks, including refusal of-administration, session commandeering and man-in-the-center attacks. ARP spoofing just takes a shot at neighborhood that utilization the Address Resolution Protocol.

DNS Server Spoofing Attacks

The Domain Name System (DNS) is a framework that partners area names with IP addresses. Gadgets that associate with the web or other private systems depend on the DNS for determining URLs, email addresses and other comprehensible space names into their relating IP addresses. In a DNS server spoofing attacks, a pernicious gathering changes the DNS server keeping in mind the end goal to reroute a particular space name to an alternate IP address. Much of the time, the new IP location will be for a server that is really controlled by the attacker and contains records tainted with malware. DNS server spoofing attacks are regularly used to spread PC worms and infections.

9. Mobile Hacking

Mobile hacking is the remote, unapproved access and control of someone else's cell phone. This sort of untrustworthy versatile hacking is commonly proficient through the abuse of deformities or glitches in portable chips or remote gadgets, for example, Bluetooth. Generally, mobile hacking is utilized to make phone calls for nothing or to accumulate individual data, for example, addresses and telephone numbers.

Ethical mobile hacking i.e., hacking accomplished with the end goal of adjusting cellular telephones emphatically - is done to anticipate remote and unapproved access to the cell phone, to alter issues or to upgrade the telephone somehow. Dishonest mobile hacking is done to assemble phone numbers and addresses for an assortment of purposes, however the most well-known objective is to charge phone calls to the hacked mobiles.

10. Cracking Passwords

Initially, we should discuss how passwords are put away. In the event that a site or program is putting away your password - like Google, Facebook or twitter that you have an online account - the password is for the most part is stored as a hash. A hash is fundamentally a protected method for putting away passwords based upon math.

A hash is likewise a method for scrambling a password - so in the event that you know the trick, you can without much of a hassle unscramble it. It is like concealing a key to your home in your front yard: on the off chance that you know where your key is, it would only take you a few moments to find it. Be that as it may, in the event that you didn't know where the key was it would likely require you a long investment to discover it.

Password attacks are divided into two types: online and offline.

Offline attacks are the place a hacker can take a password hash, duplicate it, and bring it home with them to chip away at. Online attacks require the attackers attempting to login to your online account to go to the specific website they are focusing upon.

Online attacks on secure sites are exceptionally troublesome for a hacker, on the grounds that these sorts of locales will confine the quantity of times an aggressor can attempt a password. This has likely transpired in the event that you've overlooked your password and been bolted out of your record. This framework is there to protect you from hackers who are attempting billions of suppositions to make sense of your password.

An online attack would look like if you endeavored to chase down some person's covered key in their front yard while they were home. If you looked in several spots, it doubtlessly wouldn't look too much odd; in any case, if you spent for the duration of the day preceding the house, you'd be spotted and encouraged to leave promptly!

Because of an online attack, a hacker would without a doubt do a lot of examination on a particular center to check whether they could find any recognizing information about them, for instance, birthdays, children's names, essential others, etc. Starting there, an aggressor could endeavor an unassuming group of centered passwords that would have a higher accomplishment rate than just subjective guesses.

Offline attacks are substantially more vile, and don't offer this assurance. Offline attacks happen when an encoded record, for example, a PDF or archive, is blocked, or when a hashed key is exchanged (similar to the case with Wi-Fi.) If you duplicate a scrambled document or hashed password, an attacker can bring this key home with them and attempt to break it at their recreation.

In spite of the fact that this may sound terrible, it's not as awful as you may think. Password hashes are quite often "one-path capacities." In English, this equitable implies that you can play out a progression of scrambles of your password that are alongside difficult to switch. This makes finding a password troublesome.

Basically, a hacker must be exceptionally patient and attempt thousands, millions, billions, and once in a while even trillions of passwords before they locate the right one. There are a couple ways hackers approach this to expand the likelihood that they can discover your password. These include:

  *   Dictionary Attack

Dictionary attacks are exactly what they seem like: you utilize the dictionary to discover a password. Hackers fundamentally have substantial content records that incorporate a great many nonexclusive passwords, for example, 12345, iloveyou, administrator, or 123546789.

Hackers will attempt each of these passwords - which may seem like a ton of work, yet it's most certainly not. Hackers utilize truly quick PCs (and infrequently even video games graphics cards) with a specific end goal to attempt zillions of passwords. For instance, while contending at DEFCON this last week, I utilized my design card to break a offline password, at a rate of 500,000 passwords a second!

*   Mask/Character Set Attack

On the off chance that a hacker can't figure your password from a word reference of known passwords, their next choice will be to utilize some broad tenets to attempt a considerable measure of mixes of determined characters. This implies as opposed to attempting a rundown of passwords, a hacker would determine a rundown of characters to attempt.

For instance, in the event that I knew your watchword was just numbers, I would advise my project to just attempt number mixes as passwords. From here, the system would attempt each blend of numbers until it split the watchword. Hackers can indicate a huge amount of different settings, similar to least and most extreme length, how often to rehash a particular character in succession, and some more. This declines the measure of work the project would need to do.

Along these lines, suppose I had a 8 character password made up of just numbers. Utilizing my representation card, it would take around 200 seconds- - a little more than 3 minutes- - to break this password. Be that as it may, if the watchword included lowercase letters and numbers, the same 8 character password would take around 2 days to unravel.

*   Bruteforce

On the off chance that an attacker has had no fortunes with these two strategies, they may likewise "bruteforce" your password. A bruteforce tries each character mix until it gets the password. For the most part, this sort of attack is illogical, however - as anything more than 10 characters would take a huge number of years to make sense of!

11. Trojans & Backdoors

Trojans and Backdoors are sorts of Bad-wares which their primary design is to send and get information and particularly summons through a port to another framework. This port can be even an outstanding port, for example, 80 or an out of customary ports like 7777. The Trojans are more often than not mutilated and appeared as a real and safe application to urge the client to execute them. The primary characteristic for a Trojan is that first it ought to be executed by the client, second sends or get information with another framework which is the assailant's framework.

Infrequently the Trojan is consolidated with another application. This application can be a flash card, a patch for OS, or even an antivirus. Be that as it may, really the record is worked of two applications which one of them is a safe application, and the other one is the Trojan file.

To define it, a Trojan horse is "a malevolent and security-breaking program which is outlined as something kindhearted". Such a project is intended to bring about harm, information spillage, or make the casualty a medium to attack another framework.

A Trojan will be executed with the same benefit level as the client who executes it; in any case the Trojan may abuse vulnerabilities and increment the benefit.

A critical point is that not just the association can be online (so that the orders or information are transmitted quickly between the hacker and casualty), additionally the correspondence can be disconnected and performed utilizing messages, HTTP URL transmits or as the like.

A backdoor is an uncommon way which an assailant can utilize it to get into the framework. Typical clients use login boxes and password secured approaches to utilize the framework. Indeed, even system administrator may add some security components to this framework to make it more ensure, yet the attacker can undoubtedly utilize introduced indirect access to get into framework with no password or verification.

A backdoor is a malicious PC program that is utilized to give the attacker unapproved remote access to a traded off PC framework by misusing security vulnerabilities. A Backdoor works out of sight and escapes the client. It is fundamentally the same as other malware infections and, subsequently, is entirely hard to distinguish. A backdoor is a standout amongst the most unsafe parasite sorts, as it gives a malignant individual capacity to play out any conceivable activities on a traded off PC. The attacker can utilize backdoor to keep an eye on a client, deal with his/hers documents, introduce extra hacking or hazardous dangers, control the whole PC framework and attack different hosts. Frequently a backdoor has extra ruinous capacities, for example, keystroke logging, screenshot taker, document contamination and encryption. Such parasite is a blend of various protection and security dangers, which chips away at its own particular and doesn't require to be controlled by any stretch of the imagination.

Most backdoors are pernicious projects that must be some way or another introduced to a PC. All things considered, a few parasites don't require the establishment, as their parts are as of now incorporated into software that is running on a remote host. Developers here and there leave such indirect accesses in their product for diagnostics and investigating purposes. Be that as it may, hackers use them just to break into the system.

As a rule, backdoors are particular viruses, keyloggers, trojans, spyware and remote organization apparatuses. They work in the same way as viral applications do. Although, their capacities and payload are substantially more mind boggling and unsafe, so they are assembled into one special class.

Tools examples: Brutus, Rainbow Crack, Wfuzz, John the Ripper, etc

12. Hacking Wi-Fi Networks

A wireless network is a system that utilizations radio waves to connection PCs and different gadgets together. The execution is done at the layer 1 (physical layer) of the OSI model.

To get to a wireless network, empowered gadget, for example, a portable PC, tablet, advanced mobile phones and so forth will be required. You will need to be inside the transmission range of a wireless network access point. Most gadgets (if the wireless network alternative is turned on) will furnish you with a rundown of accessible systems. In the event that the system is not password secured, then you simply need to tap on interface. On the off chance that it is secret word secured, then you will require the watchword to obtain entrance. Since the system is effectively available to everybody with a wireless network empowered gadget, most systems are password ensured.

WEP is the acronym for Wired Equivalent Privacy. It was created for IEEE 802.11 WLAN principles. Its objective was to give the protection comparable to that gave by wired systems. WEP works by scrambling the information being transmitted over the system to keep it safe from listening in.

WPA is the acronym for Wi-Fi Protected Access. It is a security convention created by the Wi-Fi Alliance in light of the shortcomings found in WEP. It is utilized to scramble information on 802.11 WLANs. It utilizes higher Initial Values 48 bits rather than the 24 bits that WEP employments. It utilizes transient keys to scramble parcels.

WEP cracking:

Cracking is the way toward abusing security shortcomings in wireless networks and increasing unapproved access. WEP breaking alludes to misuses on systems that utilization WEP to actualize security controls. There are essentially two sorts of breaks in particular;

Inactive cracking– this sort of breaking has no impact on the system activity until the WEP security has been broken. It is hard to recognize.

Dynamic cracking– this kind of attack has an expanded burden impact on the system activity. It is anything but difficult to recognize contrasted with inactive breaking. It is more compelling contrasted with uninvolved cracking.

WEP Cracking Tools:

Aircrack– system sniffer and WEP saltine.

WEPCrack– this is an open source program for breaking 802.11 WEP mystery keys. It is a usage of the FMS attack.

Kismet-this can locator wireless networks both noticeable and shrouded, sniffer bundles and distinguish interruptions.

WebDecrypt– this apparatus utilizes dynamic lexicon attacks to break the WEP keys. It has its own particular key generator and executes bundle channels.

WPA Cracking:

WPA utilizes a 256 pre-shared key or passphrase for confirmations. Short passphrases are helpless against lexicon attacks and different attacks that can be utilized to split passwords. The accompanying instruments can be utilized to split WPA keys.

CowPatty– this device is utilized to break pre-shared keys (PSK) utilizing animal power attack.

Cain and Abel– this device can be utilized to decipher catch records from other sniffing projects, for example, wireshark. The catch records may contain WEP or WPA-PSK encoded outlines.

Denial of Service (DOS):

There are numerous routes through which a hacker can dispatch a foreswearing of administration (DoS) attack on a moment messenger client. A Partial DoS attack will bring about a client end to hang, or go through a substantial segment of CPU assets creating the framework to end up shaky.

There are numerous courses in which a hacker can bring about a refusal of administration on a moment delegate customer. One regular sort of attack is flooding a specific client with countless. The well-known texting customers contain insurance against surge attacks by permitting the casualty to disregard certain clients. Be that as it may, there are numerous apparatuses that permit the hacker to utilize numerous records all the while, or naturally make countless to fulfill the surge attack. Adding to this is the Sorts of Hacking Attack and their Counter Measure 45 actuality that once, the surge attack has begun and the casualty acknowledges what has happened, the PC may get to be lethargic. In this manner, adding the attacking client records to the disregard rundown of the moment delivery person customer might be exceptionally troublesome DoS attacks are anything but difficult to produce and extremely hard to recognize, and thus are alluring weapons for hackers. In a run of the mill DoS attack, the aggressor hub parodies its IP address and uses various middle of the road hubs to overpower different hubs with activity. DoS attacks are ordinarily used to make vital servers out of move for a couple of hours, bringing about DoS for all clients served by the server. It can likewise be utilized to upset the administrations of middle of the road switches.

13. Step-By-Step Instructions for Beginners for Hacking

Step-1: Begin with the Basics

For beginners who have almost no past information of hacking, it is constantly better to begin off from the nuts and bolts. Rather than straightforwardly figuring out how to hack, you can start researching more about points, for example, PC systems, system ports, firewalls, normal system conventions like IP location, HTTP, FTP, DNS, SMTP and so on alongside how each of those stuffs work.

You can also start to learn more about substitute working system Linux whose information turns out to be important in the field of hacking. The more you find out about the fundamentals, the all the more simple it is to discover weaknesses and device abuses. When you build up an essential comprehension of the principal ideas, you will be in a position to effectively comprehend different hacking strategies that are by and by.

Step-2: Find a Good Source to Start Learning

On the off chance that one has a considerable measure of involvement in the field of hacking, there exist such a variety of books and websites that give out important information on most recent vulnerabilities alongside conceivable approaches to adventure them. Notwithstanding, for apprentices it is elusive sources that educate hacking right from the nuts and bolts in a basic and simple to take after way.

Step-3: Learn Programming

In the event that you need to step ahead, programming is something that you can't skip down. In spite of the fact that you can undoubtedly discover a ton of readymade apparatuses and projects that let you hack effortlessly, it is constantly better to have some essential information of programming dialects like PHP and JavsScript with the goal that you will be in a position to build up your own particular devices and endeavor codes.

To what extent does it take to Master the Skills of Hacking?

Hacking is not something that can be understood or mastered overnight, you should not ever be in a rush to get going. It requires information, abilities, innovativeness, devotion and obviously the time. Contingent on the measure of exertion and devotion you put, it can take up anyplace between a few months to few years to build up all the fundamental abilities. Everybody can turn into a hacker given that they take in it from the fundamentals and construct a strong establishment. In this way, on the off chance that you need to be a hacker all you need is passion to study, a great wellspring of information that will manage you through the fundamentals and some determination.

Active Attacks

An active attack is an assault portrayed by the attacker endeavoring to break into the framework. Amid an active attack, the hacker will bring information into the framework and additionally conceivably change information inside the framework.

Types of active attacks:

   *   Masquerade Attack

In a masquerade attack, the hacker puts on a show to be a specific client of a framework to obtain entrance or to increase more noteworthy benefits than they are approved for. A masquerade might be endeavored using stolen login IDs and passwords, through discovering security holes in projects or through bypassing the verification instrument.

   *   Replay Attack

In a session replay assault, a hacker takes an approved client's log in data by taking the session ID. The interloper obtains access and the capacity to do anything the approved client can do on the site.

* Message Modification Attack

In a Message modification attack, a hacker changes parcel header locations to guide a message to an alternate goal or adjust the information on an objective machine.

In a denial of service (DoS) attack, clients are denied of access to a system or web asset. This is for the most part fulfilled by overpowering the objective with more movement than it can deal with.

In a distributed denial of service (DDoS) exploitation, vast quantities of traded off frameworks (some of the time called a botnet or zombie army) attack a solitary target.

Active attacks stand out from passive attacks, in which an unapproved party screens systems and now and again checks for open ports and vulnerabilities. The object is to pick up data about the objective and no information is changed. Be that as it may, passive attacks are regularly preliminary exercises for active asaults.

Passive Attack

A passive attack is a system assault in which a framework is checked and once in a while examined for open ports and vulnerabilities. The reason for existing is exclusively to pick up data about the objective and no information is changed on the objective.

Passive attacks incorporate dynamic surveillance and uninvolved observation. In detached surveillance, an interloper screens frameworks for weaknesses without interaction, through strategies like session capture. In active reconnaissance, the hacker draws in with the target framework through techniques like port scans.

Methods for passive attacks:

War driving distinguishes powerless Wi-Fi systems by filtering them from close-by areas with a compact radio wire. The attack is commonly done from a moving vehicle, some of the time with GPS frameworks that hackers use to plot out zones with vulnerabilities on a guide. War driving should be possible just to take an Internet association or as a preparatory action for a future assault.

In dumpster diving, intruders search for data put away on disposed of PCs and other gadgets or even passwords in trash bins. The hackers can then utilize this data to encourage secretive passage to a system or network.

A hacker may take on the appearance of an approved system client and spy without association. With that get to, a hacker may observe system activity by setting the system connector to promiscuous mode.

A passive attack appears differently in relation to a active attack, in which an intruder endeavors to adjust information on the target system or information on the way for the objective framework.

Penetration testing:

Also known as pen testing, it is the act of testing a computer system, network or Web application to discover vulnerabilities that an assailant could misuse.

Pen tests can be mechanized with software applications or they can be performed physically. In any case, the procedure incorporates gathering data about the objective before the test (observation), distinguishing conceivable section focuses, endeavoring to soften up (either for all intents and purposes or no doubt) and reporting back the discoveries.

The principle goal of penetration testing is to find out security weaknesses. A pen test can also be used to test an association's security strategy consistence, its representatives' security mindfulness and the association's capacity to distinguish and react to security episodes.

Entrance tests are once in a while called white cap attacks in light of the fact that in a pen test, the good folks are the ones trying to get in.

www.ingramcontent.com/pod-product-compliance
Lightning Source LLC
Chambersburg PA
CBHW051215050326
40689CB00008B/1321